OUT OF BREATH

NOEL WILLIAMS

Published by Cinnamon Press
Meirion House,
Glan yr afon,
Tanygrisiau
Blaenau Ffestiniog,
Gwynedd, LL41 3SU
www.cinnamonpress.com

The right of Noel Williams to be identified as author of this work has been asserted by him in accordance with the Copyright, Designs and Patent Act, 1988. Copyright © 2014 Noel Williams
ISBN: 978-1-909077-19-5

British Library Cataloguing in Publication Data. A CIP record for this book can be obtained from the British Library.

All rights reserved. No part of this publication may be reproduced, stored in a retrieval system, or transmitted in any form or by any means, electronic, mechanical, photocopying, recording or otherwise without the prior written permission of the publishers. This book may not be lent, hired out, resold or otherwise disposed of by way of trade in any form of binding or cover other than that in which it is published, without the prior consent of the publishers.

Designed and typeset in Palatino by Cinnamon Press
Cover from original artwork 'dandelion' by Godunovatatiana © Godunovatatiana , agency: dreamstime.com
Cover design by Jan Fortune

Printed in Poland

Cinnamon Press is represented in the UK by Inpress Ltd www.inpressbooks.co.uk and in Wales by the Welsh Books Council www.cllc.org.uk

Acknowledgments

Acknowledgements are due to the editors of the following publications in which some of these poems or earlier versions have appeared: *A Roof of Red Tiles (Cinnamon Press 2011), Assent, Coffee House, Dreamcatcher, Envoi, Interpreter's House, In Terra Pax (Cinnamon Press 2012), Heno, wrth Gysgu, Tonight while Sleeping (Awel Aman Tawe 2010), Iota, Matter, Jericho (Cinnamon Press 2012), Obsessed with Pipework, Orbis, Other Poetry, Poetry Nottingham, Sentinel Champions #3, Shadowtrain, The Coffee House, The Frogmore Papers, The Journal, The New Writer, The North, The Prize 2011*

(Yeovil Community Arts Association 2011), The Visitors (Cinnamon Press 2010), The Sheffield Anthology: Poems from the City Imagined (Smith/Doorstop 2012) and *Words from the Web (Global Newsbox, 2009). Seven Summers* was part of the Sheffield Haiku project, 2010.

These poems were prizewinners in competitions and have appeared on the relevant websites: *Another's Lilac* (Derby City 2007), *Before Morning Comes* (Newark Poetry Society 2010), *Consolations of the Geriatrics' Porter* (Red Shed 2009), *Erosion* (Awel Aman Tawe 2010), *Heartbeat* (John Clare Cottage 2011), *On the Verge of the M40* (New Writer 2008), *Sunburn* (Sentinel Literary Quarterly 2012), *Till Death* (Northampton Literature Group 2010), *The Price of Chocolate* (runner up, Coffee House Troubadour 2009), *Cavelleria Rusticana* (Yorkshire Poet prize, Yorkshire Open, 2010), *Signal to Noise* (Yorkshire Prize, Elmet Poetry Competition, 2012).

Three poems here emerged from the work of others: *The Edge of the Day* from *Cowdust Time*, a Radio 4 production by my colleague, Clare Jenkins; *Behind Kibuye Church* from the extraordinary compassion of Clea Koff's *The Bone Woman*; and the *Kim Phuc* sequence from Denise Chong's harrowing but uplifting *The Girl in the Picture*.

I am grateful to the Arts Council, England for supporting my work in 2009, and for my residency at Bank Street Arts Centre, Sheffield. My work has been developed or supported by the kindnesses of Ann Atkinson, whose Chopin etudes and gentle words are sadly missed, Angelina Ayers, Carole Baldock, Robbie Burton, James Caruth, John Clark, Tricia Durdey, David Harmer, Chris Jones, Jonathan Davidson, Christy Ducker, Sally Goldsmith, Wendy Klein, Pippa Little, Allison McVety, Stuart Pickford, Maurice Riordan, Seni Seneviratne, Louise Wilford, all the Tuesday Poets and, for one particular poem, Helen Farish. I am especially grateful to my editor, Jan Fortune, to Helena (Nell) Nelson of Happen*Stance*, to Ann Sansom and Peter Sansom of The Poetry Business and to the indulgence and sensitivity of *Antiphon's* co-editor, Rosemary Badcoe, for their most generous and horribly apt commentary on many of these poems.

Most important of all, this volume would not exist without the particular loves of my daughter, Natasha and of the woman who keeps my head so far above water it is rarely out of the clouds, my perplexingly wonderful wife, Carrol.

Contents

Snow on the edge	9
Tying the kite	10
Plunge	11
On the verge of the M40	12
Domestic news	13
3.16	14
Planting Dorothy's garden	15
Presumably butterflies	16
The island	17
An interlude under Vulcan	18
Fallen moon	19
Consolations of the geriatrics' porter	20
A clear sky – snowdrifts	21
Daphne	22
Pluvial	23
Of the heart	24
Sunburn	25
Walking back	26
Camberwell Beauty	27
Safe house	28
Under the bridge	29
Seven summers	30
Qwerty	31
Signal to noise	32
Skating close	33
Not translated from the Swedish	34
Refraction	35
Parents	36
Before morning comes	37
Heartbeat	38
The fire garden	39
A rose of broken stone	40

After the storm	42
Walsingham, start of a barefoot mile	43
Side road	44
Return to High Force	45
How to eat an orange	46
Another's Lilac	47
Erosion	48
Last trip to Tynemouth	49
Silent night	50
The edge of the day	51
The price of chocolate	52
BFPO	53
Till Death	
1. In Salisbury	54
2. In Kandahar	55
Kim Phuc	
1. Playground	56
2. See Kim run	57
3. A benzene and polystyrene mixture	58
4. The song of yellow skin	59
5. The fire hand	60
6. The man who called in the strike	61
Behind Kibuye church	62
Out of breath	63
Notes	64

Out of Breath

Snow on the edge

Erased, the page of landscape waits.
Old childhoods have turned each gaunt thorn
and every scar of ditch and savage edge
to anticipation.
Winter skulls overnight grow lips and brows.
Clouds sleep. The road is lost. Hills inhale.

Our breaths meld in a single thought,
that the trail here and the ossuary under the snow
and the soft fist of earth battering the sky
have that same thought:
we all breathe each other here by our thinking.

The moment stands and stares at us, two figures
on a snowscape on a moor,
first marks in a sentence.

Tying the kite

Her hand pursues the kite of him
but her hand has its own trail.
Monitoring mad paper and cane,
she's hard-rooted in the hill.

She lets out the rope,
levers the kite on a fulcrum of breath.
Tissue wings slice in the slap of noise,
whip scales of a quick, chattering tail.

Her below is his above. She barely hears
the fret of the wind wanting to rip him.
Step into the wind. Step against it.
She scours shape from thoughtless air.

Her daughters haul at her skirts,
watch love rub from her finger-tips
against the thread of their father's kite, watch
her palms bruise in bullying gale.

Their hands on their mother's must feel
the lust of the kite
flickering like a skipped stone over sunlight,
her hands unmaking knots.

Plunge

He didn't mean to lean from the caique
or astonish the pipefish that flipped like a leash
and led him down past blenny and bream,
past the green timbers,
past greasy weeds
through coils of dreamt water
under mosses of copper
where a marble face,
with one eye masked, one clear,
scarred by its drowning,
a face almost memorable,
opened its silted mouth
and spat crabs of silver
but he knew
by the blinded eye and the thin tender skin of bubbles
what it meant to say.

On the verge of the M40

Your radio has too many voices.
Switch off the phone. Take the iPod from your ear.
Wipe your life sound track. Do it. Your choice is
silence. Just silence. Listen to your fear.

This path, once crowded full of fruit and flowers
is brambled now. Dim traffic fumbles near,
winding its motorway around you now as
litter, rage and tears. Listen to your fear.

Wild garlic in the mud. There, under stones
stumbled aside, dark scrabbling threads appear.
Your toecap turns a mess of tender bones,
creaking underfoot. Listen to your fear.

The fruit was sweet. Your suit is stained and torn.
Your footsteps quiet in the quivering thorn.

Domestic news

On a lighter note, Horatio
the hedgehog trapped in a well
in Steeple Aston, Oxfordshire for seven days
appears to have gnawed the likeness of Christ
in the Ryvita his rescuers lowered yesterday
as this (enhanced) photo clearly shows.

Meteorologists predict the snowfall
in our living room will subside
before the week is out. Debate on global
warming continues in the kitchen. Hall meltwater
no longer threatens the hat stand. The cat
has moved upstairs.

Sometimes you huddle close,
the colour of my stories flickering on your throat.
Sometimes you stretch away to crochet
in the wastelands of the distant cushions,
barbarous garments falling from your fingers.
I report the day as I see it, not as it is.

Finally, our main stories again.
Horatio, it turns out, is Henrietta.
The exchange rate in the bedroom
continues to fall. Analysts predict
the coldest summer for years.
The sun, they say, will burn to dead rock
well within our lifetime.

3.16

Even the hidden slither of traffic
is night-still.
That dream again that woke me, blind,

drums in my pulse, not quite smothered in starlessness
as if a baby stopped breathing in the next room.
Only my blood, only my heart,

only the slow fumble of my foot
testing the darkness, stumbling for a fuse,
tripping on the dream that sprawls in the doorway.

Planting Dorothy's garden

I'm lit by the moon she knew, near yews she planted.

Slop basket on her arm, she drifts towards me on the stepping stones, fingering the sheaves of orchis, mosses, Lockety Goldings draped in light bracelets, as if I might beg the way from her or a halfpenny. I'm at a loss for the courtesies of her century, but her smile glosses them. She lifts a silver strawberry leaf like speculation.

She trusts my arm around the soiled skirts of the lake to her window's unlit candle. Kneeling beside the sodded wall, we knead roots of lemon thyme into the soil, scribbling with seedlings lines that'll flower right to my future.

'Sometimes,' she says, 'I have to sit. A tightening in my breast. Or sometimes in my throat.'

I know it. And I know its cureless melancholy will pitch her into this same ground. What's there to say?

Unpicked cherries shine like ideas. If I could take her hand, I would lead her past her circling of the water. Her wren's eye flicks from the black fells to the lake as if suspecting me, an untimely creature, a fantasy of the memory of her lake.

Presumably butterflies

have their own way of doing things:
they're scratches on the wind; moments.
Hitting water, they dissolve.
Creatures of playful earth reach
out and snap them.

They carry fire into the wilderness
like a church window hammered
into splinters of sky, bonfire sparks
and the white gold of childhood, trailing
light through convolvulus and briar.

I found his camera under the fence where he fell.
Cracked open. I wanted those wings rising
from him to be some sort of image. But
just developed ghosts unspooling
into summer; shaky exposures, faint black and whites.

He must have been losing it before these last stills,
breathless for each pose, each wingbeat slowing.
Struggling with clogged undergrowth,
he would dream that tortoiseshells were Lancasters,
fritillaries had Avro engines, stuttering to a rhythm

he could fix. Snatch of heather, a dogrose grappling haw,
disdainful lilac, or the evening honeysuckle, stocks –
wherever there are sudden shakes
of wasps and butterflies' applause
I want to figure what he had been. And fail.

In the wildness, perhaps, something understood him.
He had his own way of doing things.
Clearing his bedside table into a bag
I found a Kodacolour of me, net in hand,
twelve years old, dust thick as pollen on the glass.

The island

Next, I drifted to an island unlike
paradise or any gothic dream,
swollen from the ocean, a dome,
a blister of glass smooth and shining
licked by tender membranes of water.

I let the boat loose, stepped on this leviathan eye.
Underfoot, under glass, fish
fled brisk as synapses. Or sparred or fed.
A metamorphic bubble, I thought, the carapace
shucked from a monstrous crab. A lost film set.

I stretched low along that glass polyp, salt slicking
my skin from toe to ear, pressing myself
down to hear how fish sang.
Gathered under, they made me their sky.
Each swam its own melody. Each mouthed its own words.

My boat slipped away, nodding to the horizon
but I had more to hear. Angels and lions, silversides,
jacks, threadfins, wrasse and spadefish
sang of their cities, sang of desire,
pathways through pale crystal I'm yet to see.

An interlude under Vulcan

She is writing, too.
I think it's a council letter.
Her bra strap is pink, loose
as she flows through her biro
on the lawn. It's too late not to notice.

Toddlers analyse glee in the fountains.
I'm tempted to follow suit.
And tie. And business haircut.
Become barefoot in sunlight.
But you know I won't.

Folding my M&S plastic triangle
to secure crumbs, I consider
its perfect design, collapsing
light like a star at a singularity.
Her letterhead says *Housing Department*.

A couple with matching hair irritate wasps
with their Metros. There's no music
but the harmonies of laughter and haughty water.
This is a city beach.
Here, the heart rests.

She cries quietly as she punctuates,
folds the letter into her bag, calls her son,
heads past the silver billiards
of St Paul's, her bra strap cutting
hard lines in her shoulder.

Fallen moon

Where the moon dropped on us, the trench
from Elsecar to Wombwell is cut glass.
Policemen, sheep, wasps in flight, ice statues of surprise.

It clipped two cities. Here on the brink, we're
puzzled the moon is, in fact, so small,
melting as it fell. You pull my hand.

We slide like rainwater on a blade
down into gardens of zirconium,
over scrapheaps of crysolite, along the tramway

fragile as frost on a whisker.
Lunar experts and lunatics speculate
on the cause. They're all wrong.

Now the whole universe is in the dock.
Physics is shut in somebody's box.
We wonder, mist rising from our mouths,
which stars fail next.

Consolations of the geriatrics' porter

Folded like a ticket
I've a telling of love too perfect to endure,
tight beneath my clinical jacket.

In a midnight scratched by torchlight
I can tell it over the eloquent locks of the nurses' home
as I test them; over owls' stark prognoses
and over and over, turning it slick as a scalpel
or a scandal slipping from mouth to mouth.

Diluting light, the lips of the doors of the ward
slop open. A woman without legs fumbles for her name.
Like all her stories, it floats beyond her hands.

I've wheeled her from ward to ward.
Her tale turned mad but mine is certain.
The mortuary gate gives with a whisper.
I tap my pocket. I've a ticket out of here.

A clear sky – snowdrifts

You know that place where four paths meet
near the cemetery's brow, where I gaze sometimes
over the stumps of the common graves
low on the slope, or up to the shadows of angels,
with the ache behind me of the arthritic gate,
and ahead the long sleeping street
of mound after mound swollen, down
to the drop of the valley? There,

as if cupped in the calyx of the city's black flower
I stared into silence, between ice-white yews
where two headlights swept up to me,
roving the graves and strobing the drifts
from left to right, so the glide of the beams
lit up one by one each of your words
I'd shaped in the darkness of snow.

Daphne

If I was to call myself un-uprootable
you would measure the dredge
of my feet in the lakeside (where fox-colours
glide just under the glaze). You would
flick through your lexicon of trunks
and branches, testing: am I worm-filled, leaning,
am I wind-fingered and dreaming
with the madness of trees?

You would map my toes' hook, my clutch
of the mud and my stance as I'm stripped
by the wind; want to tap the resins
of surely my leaking vocabulary.
Am I rotted by autumn? Is it a fit?
A despair in the sap that forces
such forging of syllables? To
drill down and anchor, to tree me
where all leaves have dissolved on the lake bed?

If I was to call myself un-uprootable
you'd put your sole to a spade,
you'd whet each blade of your lips.

Pluvial

It rained for thirty years, and
we'd still not finished the house. Buckets,
tin trays, groundsheets all dragged into use.
It rained another ten. As the furniture
drifted through the doorway,
and the children began their circumnavigation
of the allotment, I thought of you
alone in the umbrella shop, your till anchored
so the fivers didn't float.
How we'd sailed Pooh sticks
under Sydney Harbour Bridge, wondering
if they'd reach the forests of Antarctica.

Of the heart

So you quit the page for the garden
which wears a streetlit kilt of rain.
The twist of your rib continues.
Whatever nests in that fork of bones
turns and turns like a dog after comfort.

Touch the washing line,
rhinestones strung against the garden's dark.
Raindrops arpeggio down, timed
to the tick ticking of your left arm.
The fall of this aurora, spark by spark,
troubles the mud, silver silting a vein.

Sunburn

The sun was bigger then, easily swallowed the sky,
so burning that at night there was no night,
in the swell of summer at the height of my life.
And the heat blazed back out of cornstalks and corrugated earth,
off the barn and chestnuts, elms and oaks,
smouldering up to that solder sky.

Every day I was new to the fields.
Turning and tedding the freshly mown
or straddling the baler behind the tractor
red as three fire engines, hauling out bale
after bale like squat logs, hefting them
off the conveyor, a hand slung under each twine.

That summer lasted years.
There were no rules – the future like sunburn
on my shoulders, peeling new skin,
cool pain under the skim of a single sheet
dreamless as the swifts scooping gnats
above the mud of the pond.

Knotting a headscarf over my mouth,
I stepped down the ladder into the grain bin.
It held the sunheat in its sheet steel box
a cake-tin to bake a man, lined with grain
so fine on walls and floor and clothes that it clogged
my nostrils with rich silt; a warm, perfumed frost.

I was stripped to my jeans and barefoot
sweeping dust like soot or fine plaster.
And the water was brought out to the field
in a bucket. And you threw mugfuls over me
streaking the grime off my back, making tears of my face
on the hot straw you laid under the hedge.

Walking back

Birdsong creaks and falters, steel
on glass. Sky grey as skin.
Under bramble I probe half
a coffee cup, walk on.
Rooks settle over the melting path,
sneer, chuckle in soft-focus.

I'm slow up the curve of the ridge
into the rustle of allotments, interrogating
half-fallen sheds. My knee folds
to the slope. I count neon and TV blues
through the Vaseline of evening.
Here's where you stood for the photo.

That might be a fox in a clutch of elder, stiff.
Or you – marking astrology
in streetlights, testing the stones' comfort,
goading me to wedge our fingers
under a tilted door in the hawthorn,
tramp into someone's broad beans and Helenium.

Stretched in a snag of beech or lime
ghost plastic rattles, lifts.
Evening, says a stranger.
We're shadows to each other.
You run. He's gone. Etched
on bare branches frost gets first grip.

Camberwell Beauty

After the waters close, I go back home, dive in.
I swim the old walks, the drowned hills of Loxley,
slow breast-stroke through branches of the birch
I never climbed. A crab back-flips
in the fronds of our dandelion garden
where eel and flat fish burgle cucumber frames.

My tricycle's coral but the bell still rings,
its bubbles of tin plodding through flood
to startle a seahorse from the osiers
I'd stripped for my arrows and bow
when I was Robin Hood and Geronimo.
Now sharks stalk gilled finches in the haw.

There's still a point in breathing. I jack-knife
through railings we bent in strong-arm games,
up through warm-water woods,
surface in waves of church-glass.
Red Admirals, Tortoiseshells, Camberwell Beauties
petal new sea, drowned in light.

Safe house

It wakes and wants you.
It prowls from bowl to bowl.
It roughs itself up on pebble-dash.
The moon may be full now, but you are all it wants.

I think you left the door unhinged.
I think the floorboards need a fix.
I think the fridge is humming. It may have spilled itself.
It doesn't sound innocent to me.

I think the radiator is in heat.
I think these sheets are sweating.
I think the light-bulb has given up the ghost.
I think the clock's alarmed.

It noses the torn carpet.
It brushes the candles out.
It needs no map and no dictionary.
It wakes and it wants you.

Under the bridge

It was not the last day I rode that bike,
my hands tacked to plastic, bell big as an apple,
the sun oozing over the embankment
to make toffee of the tarmac.

Not the last day of summer I'd scoot under my bridge
where the road tipped into darkness,
plough the red wheels up the roadside dump of gravel,
wheels drowning, shovelling, stuck.

It was not the last day wild grit
sprayed up to my knees as I heard
tractors joust beyond the embankment,
rooks spar and flap with the racket of parents.

It was the day I understood *now* slides
in tiny stones. Coming home
to no radio by the sink, her empty coat hook,
Dad gripping the puncture kit with meticulous fury.

Seven summers

Sucking sweet green blades.
My towel damp under me.
The Secret Seven.

Jeans greased by the chain,
I balance her birthday horse
on the handlebars.

Dead Man's Pool. The pole
hooked in mermaid weeds. We drift.
Willow flecks her eyes.

I breathe concrete, fold
my eyes under the sun's weight.
Gold stone. Fat brick. Noon.

A cocked flowerpot.
Buddleia snoring with bees.
A melted cat yawns.

Umbrellas roof our
barbecue in a hailstorm.
Steaks cooked by lightning.

A blackbird, a breeze,
the sudden pulse of roses.
Song my pen forgets.

Qwerty

Standing behind you as you type
my shape irritates your screen.
Juniper lifts from your neck like heat,
your shoulder warm as snow.

The pelt of the keyboard purrs to your touch.
I lift your fallen shawl. You slow,
shrug it back, squint at a comma,
shepherd vagrant hair.

I cannot read those other lives
you live, the children and lovers
of your fingertips. Their valeta,
the curve of their gravities,

their roman candles of bewilderment
are occult as your DNA or first love.
Perhaps I seek your comfort
from what I might see on the screen.

Low and gold the sun flares
through bare horse chestnuts, gilding
frost, drowning reflections in flame.
I'll draw the curtains.

Signal to noise

On a stack of paperbacks the radio tilts.
I reach it after the bedside light.

Sometimes, unplugged, for a while
a Tallis melody remains, a fade of voices.

I curl round this metaphor.
On valves you could warm your hands like a fireside

their filaments caterpillar flame in a mahogany box
solid as the knowledge of cornflakes, pressed sheets,

Robin Hood Saturdays, a warm hearth in the morning.
Solder on a nib of iron in teardrop silver

would burn off as he plugged resistor to capacitor
built a radio of germanium and brittle board

for my bedside. I've his tapes, too.
Hancock, Kenneth Horne, other dead voices

pretending childhood was real. But its castle
had no walls, no roof. And when I wandered off

cat at my heels, knotted handkerchief slung
I'd no idea the road turned back on itself.

As valves cool their glow drains,
voices decline,
though sound stays faster than light.

Skating close

Fractured beneath the ice, his face,
his fingers, grind against it.
I don't fear him. Look –
if I leap or stamp, he flips away,
defeated.
Though too quickly he's back,
glittering fly at a sweetshop window.

Over his eyes I etch sentences
out of his grasp.
There – as I slide over him – there –
an angel in my ether:
my score deletes his every sign.

There. Watch them flinch. And there:
slurs of ice shearing,
confetti sprinkling the veil of feeling.

I'd know my own reflection if I saw it.

Let him bring
amphibian bit and brace, trepan the pond,
insinuate this ghost-breathing.
My blades will slit his hands.
I'll weld his hot lips to the whispering ice.

Not translated from the Swedish

The black lip of the sky presses
the white lip of the sea.

She squats on bruised heels at the crucifix
of the shore, spine to the wind, preening bouquets

razor shell by shell to shred the waves' petticoat.
She winds her hair with bladderwrack, writes

a frost of salt round her throat,
puts a pure nub of some stone or other in her mouth.

With bare thighs, she fills her skirt
one pebble at a time.

Refraction

Under cravats and bowties I can't have worn, surely,
a glass heart sulks in this full, stuck drawer,
evidence of times I no longer believe,
like the crack in the door she kicked in
to force final words from me. Can I even be sure
she had eighteen years here? These summer-lit photos
are probably fakes. Yet three undead cacti
stuffed in a jug prickle with proof of her.

Slow subsidence worms under the mud.
Too readily slates seem to slide from the roof.
Assurances, mementoes, every certificate
of cider in blackouts, punts on the backs,
barefoot tennis, cruising the night after gigs,
feels forged, and every witness a ghost
snatching at loose spills of memory
to find her name on a headstone, her face
in a snapshot or a stamp on a letter
still scented with Cutt's Market oranges
I'd peeled as I first slit the seal of her overture
which here in my hand feels a fiction
she'd nurtured to puzzle me, why me,
why a heart of glass, why was I
drawn into her black nets,
stockings laid over strawberries to keep
the fruit sweet and beaks and claws out?

Parents

For a while they walk where they used to be.
You see them in old places,
reflected in Debenhams' window,
in the avoiding turn of a head,
as the flash of a ring in a crowd
thick on a nicotined finger.

Slowly they abandon those places
to crouch in shadowed lanes of the heart,
alleys of almost forgetting,
thinned like the mornings of childhood
under the noon stare.

There they dream
they may take your hand again
and squeeze it white
in one iced moment of unwanted remembering.

Do you want to be where we are?
Do you want us to close you in the hollow of our arms?
Do you yet believe it truly happened?

Are you still building bricks by the fireplace
thinking we've stepped out to warm the beds?

Before morning comes

Once, aged fourteen, I unlatched my bedroom window,
stepped naked onto the roof of our porch,
crouched on the concrete in starlight.

Night ran summer fingers over me,
licked the lidless windows of the sleeping street
in that flat town south of Banbury.

Across the road a sash slid up.
A girl, naked as a mirror, stumbled out,
clinging to the creeper at her ledge.

All along the street the young left warm families for sodium light,
cowed on garage roofs, the rose trellis, the bay;
some in tears, some trying to speak, bereft in new skin.

In those days the milkman would slip a yoghurt pot
over each bottle to stop the morning blue-tits.
Sometimes it would topple, smash and spill.

Heartbeat

If you wake expecting you never would,
despite tubes in your neck, the drain
in your chest, the creak of your breastbone,
the buzz of demons dipped in morphine, you'll smile.

Some days celebrate themselves simply because
the sun decides to rise
a nurse straightens her stocking
a child climbs on a bed where he thought he'd said goodbye.

Today the wheels of the chair squeal like cheerleaders
as we steer down the ambulance ramp.
Today rain thrashes cymbals in the sycamores
and tickertape leaves fall in applause.

Today at the lily by our door,
before turning the key, you touch my shoulder.
Rainwater weeps off the hawthorn.
Our lawn glitters with a carpet of may.

The fire garden

Where she walks
roses turn towards her.
If she smiles,
they burn.

When she bows or bends
to tap the soil around tinder,
flame fingers its way from the earth.

She buries cinders for seeds,
harvests an orange too gold to peel,
bites a peach of ginger snow,
spits stones of fire melting.

The breeze from the west lifts sparks from the thorn
scattering on the neighbours' sky.
As she waits for her man of rime,
at her feet a tortoiseshell flares.

A rose of broken stone

you choose soft focus
a swan nests in plastic
below the cliffs

I'm three steps behind
on the walls of the headland
holding back storm

cliff-top silhouette
sheer path to faded saints
a bindweed climb

camera ready
we trample foxgloves
to reach the ruin

mud – a willow plugs
the fallen gate: we cup hands
in the rusted pool

our crumpled guidebook
a thrush knocks rain from its branch,
stains the chapel floor

roots in the fireplace
a rift where children crouched –
rooks in the chimney

a nave of alder
in the shadow of angels
perspective vanishes

rain on broken glass
wings in the wet slant of evening
your lens cracked

carved stars and roses
grey ribbed chancel wall
in a pool of the moon

graves scoured by sea-wind
cold charcoal of a tramp's fire
holy words erased

page-white stone
long steps to the roof
your spray-can rattle

ancient voices
caught in the vault – we shout
back at ourselves

down the cellar's dark
my fist holds a broken rose
these steps lead one way

in silent lightning
the abbey's eyeless window
dead stars – a black cloth

After the storm

Later, the slide of snowmelt off the gutter
crumbling onto moonlight brings back the hiss
of your touch on the cymbals' ride and crash
when you tamped the snare with your sleeve.

When ice squeals, it's those van doors.
The wind breathes like a bass drum roped to the roof rack
straining as you gunned it up the M6,
to the blizzard screaming for your autograph.

An icicle cracks. The snap
of one white stick riddles darkness
with brittle clumps of snow, a line
of lights dissolving in pitter-patter silence.

The attic is bleached of flam and paradiddle.
I'm at the window in a silvered room.
Radio and TV play white noise.
Both phones are still.

Walsingham, start of a barefoot mile

She chooses a candle in red glass.
Not pelican blood. Not Pentecostal fire.
The ruby of a girl's first lipstick,
flickering two hundred kisses on the wall.
Heat churns off wicks fierce as faith.

I can't see it.
Yes, quiet. Yes, you take
your flame from the wax of a stranger.
Yes, there's one light always
though each separate candle fails.

But I hear the mower
sneering its green stripes
beyond the ancient cartoon window.
What's the need for a votive lawn
if you're walking barefoot upon flints?

Side road

As I drive from the city
lights failing behind
mist distils from the night,
moth-wings of darkness.

At forty mph the car stands still
and the windscreen rhythm
pumping two fingers at the hidden world
is all that's awake.

I'm tempted to power down and pull over
drop the window, sip on stars
though there are no stars,
strip to the air if it will have me.

I douse the headlights.
Ghosts slide on the skin of the Zafira.
Two bloodshot lights flare from the road
head high, startled in the dark, red holes.

Afterwards, I must have swerved,
there's nothing under my torch.
Sheep are nudging a crusted hedge.
I think that's a blackbird fluttering.

Return to High Force

Stretched out with your Kodak you lean beyond the brink
as if gravity's keener over the fall, tilted to dive.
In that furious sluice you could relapse
for a few free moments of unearthly drop
that might elide the torrent in your head
in the hurl and mercy of the cascade.

Instead you toss down one by one, her phrases
cold as farthings, nothing coins,
spinning into white noise until you can't tell
if they're the glint of birds sniping or hooked fish
or deceits from that voice beguiling as candlelight
whose whisper won't drown.

You're on your own. Down to the pool.
Desire ebbs here to quiet
sidling through bracken laced by the shawl of spray.
Somehow the shout and hooligan of water
becomes puzzled by the trees, browses now
shyly, sliding by half-fallen pine, dark under skirts of larch.

Half-hid, wrapped over rocks wrecked in the Pleistocene
a silhouette stares across the water
long fingers drawling the wet, a kelpie draped in shadow.
That's when you recall the camera still wedged above the falls
if not yet nicked with all it holds. The figure shifts,
ripples turning from the lazy hand, as if to speak
or to hear a new voice.

How to eat an orange

Simply cut in clean half with a sharp knife.
Or segments, each hived with juice

as at Candytown or from my mother's hand
before her arthritis. With skill you can skin

the whole flesh in one spiral. If so, thrown over
the shoulder, it'll tell your future bed-mate.

If the fruit's full of pips, you'll need to spit
or press them from your lips to the bin.

Either way, don't let the seed into your gut.
It may sprout and flower. All your arteries

will leaf into orangeries, your blood
become so sweet it can be squeezed onto pancakes

so you'll seek only sunlight and scented rain
and dream you had no other dream.

Another's Lilac

Its scent is its colour,
    thickened
        to still me,
as I'm night-walking.

Preening strangers' hedgerows, a thief
    for black lilac.
           Already,
                stars.

Shadow
    fattens the scent.
Perhaps a woman's passing, her
                evoked throat: sole amethyst
leafed in jet on silver wire.

Night ripples –
    fingering the silks.
           If I'd a home:

this garden, this woman.

Erosion

Sunlight once slid heartsong into the slow,
steady falls of water. My circumstance
deluded then, perhaps. Or does it now?
Young brick, old hill: the same indifference.

Childhood clouds swarmed those hilltops, stained the rock.
Rills necklaced them with glass, scoured brackened routes
through blackened peat, frost, sullen slugs of fog
but all they told me then were platitudes.

Now where the birch is steel; fell, pre-stressed shell;
roots, concrete; memory swells to myth,
stretches my city's chrysalis until
the landscape creaks and something has to give.

Cashpoint, suburb, office block, car park: all
slide with the hillside into the waterfall.

Last trip to Tynemouth

East seawind scoured these headstones
into Hepworths and Moores, ribbed, rutted anatomies.
We picnic in their lee, under the Priory tower
cracked against clouds like a parable.

I've cress and egg. You've parma ham. Your hair
streams like kelp in a dragging tide.
You trace the stats on sandstone
find hints of a name that might be ours.

I snap my Braeburn's stalk, toss it,
watch it dither, harried over the cliff
buttoning myself against the flit of Easter shadows
although there's comfort somehow in the chill.

We seem to belong. Perhaps past visits with the kids
call antiphony from weary stone.
A crow lands in the lancet, black against blue.
The damp's getting through your slacks.

We harvest litter, stuff our bags. On my knees
I tuck the apple core into a grave.
The outlines of our bodies on the grass
perfect as the wind gets up.

Silent night

The black sky is yellow.
Siren-quiet. Silent as a mob of drunks.
LED, sodium, plasma, neon.
The domed meniscus of the city.

Through my arteries a train
bumps its coaches over glitches in the rail.
Ber-dum.
There's another on the viaduct. *Ber-dum.*

I used to ride.
Flinging, leaping, scribbling, grinning.
Ber-dum.
I ate destinations.

Turning in the sheet, tender inch by inch.
Testing my progress against
the strain of breath
and your warm dreams.

A swill of blood in my forehead.
Copper and silver spilled
by street on duvet. *Ber-dum.*
Count the pieces.

The edge of the day

Everything happens in dusk.
Silk dust shawls the children
filling the goat-track with that old rhyme,
their song shuffling cows to the barn
under the shoulders of the sun.
What have I been today? What have I become?

Rooks annotate scribbled trees.
In the scrub a dog lifts its nose
to cedar smoke, squinting.
Grandmother with her peacock feather
whisks away demons, wide-eyed
at stars flaring red in the shadow of earth.

The price of chocolate

As usual, the scratch of gunfire in the undergrowth
taunts our patrol. My gun rests loose in its sling.

As usual, Serbs sprawl at their checkpoint
eyeing ill-hidden mines. They know
we can kick them aside. They need their ritual.

The one with the words is not the leader.
As usual, negotiation.

One of them cracks through the hedge,
drags out that girl we've seen before,
twelve or thirteen, his hand wound in her hair.

Younger than my cousin, she crawls before him.
Frost sprinkles them from the briar.
Our standing orders: let these things go.
There'll be others like her. She isn't Lianne.

But there is a glade in her eyes.
I see jackdaw secrets.
I speak hard. Frost crusts each mine
cold as our broken languages.

A carton of Silk Cut is the price of
shoving the dumb bombs aside.
A kitkat and eight smokes from an opened pack enough
to send her scooting back to the woods,
treasuring her bruises for the hoard.

BFPO

She counts today's eggs and waters the milk.
Her cheeks are mapped with broken veins.
She stops a whisper on her lips.
She waits at the window as the sun begins.

She leans at the door all day ajar.
She strokes her throat where the necklace lay.
She opens the letter with a butter knife.
Her eyes are melted tar.

She shovels earth for a frozen bird.
She sees a starving horse in a field.
She bathes in ice.
She shrouds the clock that screamed in the night.

Till Death

1. In Salisbury

What was severe is comfort now:
the TV being quiet Saturday,

those same two lager cans each week
iced deeper into the fridge.

Frost can be solace, as if, in time,
it will mass to sweetness. They say

if you sleep in snow you grow warm.
I wonder about the sound of bullets.

Will he tell me, is a pin hammer clipping brick
not being dead yet; the club of a fist

slapping wet sand the first clue to pain?
I wish sometimes to hear his flesh leak

bringing its drone of homecoming.
If he leaves blood behind, I'll still drink all he holds.

On the fridge door I mark each day in magnets.
In this slow silence each click is a trigger.

2. In Kandahar

Some count the months. Some days. Or hours.
They think it's normal, here

behind rocks rich as a vein in the eye,
a ruin shot with blood.

Secrets breed in rock.
A stranger discovers his place in no-place:

a land of stones tipped on pivots of stone,
mounted by a stone sun.

In this salt heat my true love sleeps
steel in my arm's crook, wordless as a wound.

My eye had not sighted on love at first
till she simplified our ruin with blood.

Her sweat is oil on my hands.
I've filed off safety. Upon my chest

lies her absolute trust, for I'll carry and keep her
as we make room for other lives.

I don't count days. Time is solid as stone.
I count enemies, cold.

Kim Phuc

1. Playground

Pocking dust in the yard
rain hits the treetops hard and fast.
She's first to laugh and last
parting the feathered grass to race
for shelter under laced
papaya palms, each space a sheen
of water, bright and green.
In leaflight, barely seen, the boys
snatch twigs, snarling the noise
of guns, jabbing their toys. She falls.
A smile graces her. All
she hears is their harsh call, the rain,
thunder crackling like pain.
Lightning descends again. And hard.

2. See Kim run

I am a princess. I am Lieu Hanh
with pearls strung in waterfalls from my waist.
I dance among pigs, rooting
in split pink guava. With Grandma Tao
I fold sticky rice in betel leaves.
I wake Grandpa with drips from the hose.

Why would the world drown me in fire
to make me change it? My ponytail fell
in the ash of cousin Danh.
Childhood burned off my back.
My country swelled from a single street
to every island and skin of soil.

But I don't want to live there.
When bombs fall, we run from
and into hands melting around us.
I am a princess of waterfalls and pigs.
I want to be cool under papaya and palm,
running into rain.

3. A benzene and polystyrene mixture

benzene burns
you can use gasoline, petrol
dissolve styrofoam in it
the mix sticks to anything
it's easy as making rice biscuits

in the warm junglesafe temple calm
of the hidden afternoon
people discovered they were matters of fact
with the startled look
of spent matches

you run for anywhere the fire is not
you run for the trees
but the trees are kindling
you run for the river
but the water rises in steam
you run for home
but home is running from you
you run for her arms

a line of silence

4. The song of yellow skin

When you see the flame the bomb has already fallen.
Earth has shifted irrevocably. Every bright bird is
caught, singing the song of Yellow Skin.

Napalm eats history, all that is gold and green,
snatches the sun down to melt in Kim's nerves.
Now she can translate the unspeakable

each creak of her healing skin whispers ash,
the only eulogy for her cousins.
Her home, veined with weeds

traps a black bird in concrete
fluttering in its ruin. She is crying
with the door shut, ragging feathers on cement.

5. The fire hand

Though my prayers move from house to house
in our church which is nowhere,
I have always the same Amen:
forgive those who trespassed against me,
and let a door open to a home without whispers,
where I choose my own words, or silence.

Let no-one script my nightmares.
Let me bind those bleeding,
help them believe in a new skin.
Give us our own chance to fill rifles.
with forget-me-nots, grenades with rue.
I know what war is.

It stalks like a forest fire as you flee in your sleep.
So you run to outstretched hands,
no more the hands of Lieu Hanh, ghost princess,
but long fingers bullet-hard. Under her fingernails
the pith of greenskinned oranges,
on her palm a scar where heart and lifeline cross.

6. The man who called in the airstrike

Awake, she says it's okay.
She has to suffer like that.

Like a paper doll burned to the ancestors
she is smoke curling up,
she has an edge of hot light.
Whom she touches burns.

Still, he seeks her hand.

Behind Kibuye church

Considering this slope of bone and rag
you have to find your breath. You must
transcribe these dead.

You can unwind an ulna from its black sleeve
bag it in plastic, mark it on the hill.
Flag by flag you map and fillet broken trails

in red. Against each gold palm
people were unfolded, cut, emptied into fern.
Now they open their mouths to you.

The light flows up
as you turn each face to cloud,
each wound to the earth

while the arch of rain holding this thin sky fades
under the persistence of flies,
the slice of the machete.

Out of breath

They've burned my books, newspaper,
flowers, clothes, money, pen.
The room is antiseptic.
It may be Thursday.

In gloves and a gown the colour of calm
she brings her machine to my bedside
to calibrate my lungs.
She protects herself with brisk apology,
seals her notes.
No matter how hard it is to breathe
the machine wants more.

I pace slow lino barefoot,
cherish the cold on my sole
that tests my fallible chest.
I listen to the surgeon whittling old bones,
wonder what I can make
of the one thing I have left.

Notes

'Planting Dorothy's Garden' p. 15 Dorothy Wordsworth's journals not only guided her brother's poems, but continue to spark contemporary writers, too. Lockety Goldings are either the globe flower or possibly marigolds.

'An Interlude under Vulcan' p. 18 A statue of Vulcan stands on the dome of the Town Hall in Sheffield.

'Walsingham, start of a barefoot mile' p. 43 Walsingham has been a site of pilgrimage since 1061 when the chapel of the Holy House was erected, apparently through a miracle.

'BFPO', 'Till Death' the 'Kim Phuc' sequence & 'Behind Kibuye church' pp. 52-62 These ten poems evolved from a Residency at Bank Street Arts Centre, Sheffield. One strand of the work explored women's experience of war.

'Kim Phuc' sequence pp. 56-61 Phan Thi Kim Phuc is a Vietnamese woman who, when she was nine, was severely burned in a South Vietnamese napalm attack in 1972. The image of her pain, starkly recorded in Nick Ut's iconic photograph, may indirectly have helped shorten the Vietnam War. She now runs the Kim Phuc Foundation, a charity helping children affected by war. Details in these poems are drawn from Denise Chong's *The Girl in the Picture*.

'Playground' p. 56 This poem uses the Vietnamese form *luc bat* (meaning "six-eight").

'Behind Kibuye church' p. 62 The source of this poem is Clea Koff's *The Bone Woman*. In it she records with harrowing objectivity her forensic investigations of mass killings in Rwanda, Bosnia, Croatia and Kosovo.

ENDORSEMENTS

Once Upon a Deal... reveals that effective negotiation is an art, showcasing how creativity, fresh approaches and listening with a curious and open mind can lead to success.
Ruth Buchanan – Commercial Support Lead, John Lewis & Partners

Investing in negotiation training with Scotwork has been a game-changer for our business. With around 50% of our team trained, we've not only strengthened our confidence when negotiating with much larger customers but have also shifted to a position of strength – fully understanding and articulating the value we bring.

The impact has been tangible and immediate. In just six months post-training, we successfully closed one of the largest deals in our company's history and increased our profitability by tens of thousands of pounds. The insights, strategies and mindset shift we gained through this programme have transformed how we approach negotiations, and the results speak for themselves.

I highly recommend Scotwork to any organisation looking to elevate their negotiation skills and drive meaningful business outcomes.
Sheri Hickok – CEO, Climate Impact Partners

As a fan of negotiation theory and a lover of great storytelling, *Once Upon a Deal...* makes the theory really come alive through entertaining and compelling anecdotes. From negotiating with the EU to negotiating with your mother, and from negotiating the price of a hotel room to negotiating with your dog to keep him from chasing grouse, this book shows how having a solid negotiation plan will always get you better results.

Once Upon a Deal... will show you how to think like Stephen Hawking and Abraham Lincoln and even show you how to negotiate a gold medal at the Olympic Games. It takes academically-proven theory, on which Scotwork's world-class training is based, and illuminates the theory through a wonderful collection of stories. You'll earn the price of the book back a thousand-fold!

Ben Fricke – Global Procurement Director, Whitbread

An outstanding compilation that allows us to draw up the experiences of others to help with your own negotiation journey.

Bobby Singh - SVP, Global Commercial Officer, WPP

As a publisher, I believe in the power of storytelling and *Once Upon a Deal...* applies this most effective tool to the art of negotiation. These stories, distilled from years of knowledge and application, and told in an engaging, absorbing manner, will enhance any reader's skills in this area.

David Young - Retired CEO of Hachette Book Group, USA